# KEEP
# CALM
## SURE
## IT'LL BE
# GRAND

KEEP CALM SURE IT'LL BE GRAND

With research by Stephen Brownlee and Laura Holden

Summersdale Publishers Ltd
46 West Street
Chichester
West Sussex
PO19 1RP
UK

www.summersdale.com

Printed and bound in China

ISBN: 978-1-84953-302-7

Substantial discounts on bulk quantities of Summersdale books are available to corporations, professional associations and other organisations. For details telephone Summersdale Publishers on (+44-1243-771107), fax (+44-1243-786300) or email (nicky@summersdale.com).

# KEEP
# CALM
## SURE
## IT'LL BE
# GRAND

summersdale

There are only
two kinds of people
in the world: the Irish
and those who wish
they were.

**Anonymous**

We may have bad weather
in Ireland, but the sun
shines in the hearts of the
people and that keeps
us all warm.

**Marianne Williamson**

An Irishman will always
soften bad news, so that a
major coronary is no more
than 'a bad turn'.

Hugh Leonard

The only thing
that has to be finished
by next Friday is
next Thursday.

**Maureen Potter**

A life spent making mistakes
is not only more honourable,
but more useful than a life
spent doing nothing.

**George Bernard Shaw,**
*The Doctor's Dilemma*

Try not to worry…
take each day just one
anxiety attack at
a time.

Tom Wilson

Life's a tough proposition,
and the first hundred years
are the hardest.

**Wilson Mizner**

Never hit an Irishman when he's down. He might get up again.

Seamus O'Leary

If at first you don't succeed,
try, try again. Then quit.
No use being a damn
fool about it.

W. C. Fields

Everything is funny as long as it is happening to somebody else.

**Will Rogers**

# Life is just one damned thing after another.

**Elbert Hubbard**

One may walk over
the highest mountain one
step at a time.

John Wanamaker

Other people have a
nationality. The Irish…
have a psychosis.

Brendan Behan

Nostalgia isn't what
it used to be.

**Anonymous**

It is always the best policy to speak the truth – unless, of course, you are an exceptionally good liar.

Jerome K. Jerome

The world is
disgracefully managed,
one hardly knows to
whom to complain.

Ronald Firbank

This is one race of
people for whom
psychoanalysis is of
no use whatsoever.

**Sigmund Freud on the Irish**

You may not realise it when
it happens, but a kick in the
teeth may be the best thing
in the world for you.

**Walt Disney**

Being Irish, he had an abiding sense of tragedy, which sustained him through temporary periods of joy.

**William Butler Yeats**

Anywhere you go liking
everyone, everyone
will be likeable.

Mignon McLaughlin

No life is so hard
that you can't make it
easier by the way
you take it.

**Ellen Glasgow**

One of the best lessons you can learn in life is to master how to remain calm.

Catherine Pulsifer

All I want to do is sit
on my arse, fart and
think of Dante.

Samuel Beckett

We don't have anything
as urgent as *mañana*
in Ireland.

**Stuart Banks**

Never worry
about your heart till
it stops beating.

E. B. White

Have patience with all
things, but chiefly have
patience with yourself.

St Francis de Sales

When anyone asks me about the Irish character, I say look at the trees. Maimed, stark and misshapen, but ferociously tenacious.

Edna O'Brien

There is no
failure except in no
longer trying.

Elbert Hubbard

Love is never defeated, and I could add, the history of Ireland proves it.

Pope John Paul II from a speech to the people of Galway, September 1979

Even if you fall on your face, you're still moving forward.

Robert Gallagher

An Irishman can be worried
by the consciousness that
there is nothing to
worry about.

**Austin O'Malley**

Accept the impossible, do without the indispensable and bear the intolerable.

Kathleen Norris

Storms make oaks
take deeper root.

George Herbert

Ireland is where strange
tales begin and happy
endings are possible.

**Charles Haughey**

Be like a duck. Calm on the surface, but always paddling like the dickens underneath.

**Michael Caine**

The man who
smiles when things go
wrong has thought
of someone to
blame it on.

Robert Bloch

The Irish people
do not gladly suffer
common sense.

Oliver St John Gogarty

Every now and then go
away, have a little relaxation,
for when you come back to
your work your judgment
will be surer.

Leonardo da Vinci

A truly happy person
is one who can enjoy
the scenery while on
a detour.

**Anonymous**

The Irish, with their glowing hearts and reverent credulity, are needed in this cold age of intellect and scepticism.

Lydia Child

Start by doing what's necessary; then do what's possible; and suddenly you are doing the impossible.

**St Francis of Assisi**

# Success is due less to ability than to zeal.

**Charles Buxton**

To be Irish is to know that
in the end the world will
break your heart.

Daniel Patrick Moynihan

Tough times never
last. Tough people do.

Robert Schuller

It just wouldn't be
a picnic without
the ants.

**Anonymous**

I have a simple philosophy:
fill what's empty, empty
what's full and scratch
where it itches.

Alice Roosevelt Longworth

# Life is either a daring adventure or nothing.

**Helen Keller**

If you're lucky enough
to be Irish, then you're
lucky enough.

**Irish proverb**

The robbed that smiles,
steals something from
the thief.

William Shakespeare, *Othello*

Therefore, do not be anxious about tomorrow, for tomorrow will be anxious for itself. Let the day's own trouble be sufficient for the day.

Matthew 6:34

There is no language
like the Irish for
soothing and quieting.

John Millington Synge

One doesn't discover new lands without consenting to lose sight of the shore for a very long time.

André Gide

It has been my
philosophy of life that
difficulties vanish
when faced boldly.

**Isaac Asimov**

May those who love us love us,
And those that don't love us,
May God turn their hearts.
And if He doesn't turn their hearts,
May he turn their ankles,
So we'll know them by their limping.

**Irish curse**

The problem with
some people is that
when they aren't
drunk, they're sober.

W. B. Yeats

Adversity has ever been
considered the state in
which a man most easily
becomes acquainted
with himself.

Samuel Johnson, *The Rambler*

God is good,
but never dance in
a small boat.

**Irish proverb**

A lament in one ear,
maybe, but always
a song in the other.

Sean O'Casey

May the enemies of Ireland never eat bread nor drink whiskey, but be afflicted with itching without the benefit of scratching.

**Irish curse**

Life is not meant to
be easy, my child, but
take courage: it can
be delightful.

George Bernard Shaw,
*Back to Methuselah*

If you want to be happy, be.

Leo Tolstoy

A certain amount of
opposition is a great help
to a man. Kites rise against
and not with the wind.

**John Neal**

It's a long road that
has no turning.

**Irish proverb**

Problems are opportunities
with thorns on them.

Hugh Miller

That's the Irish people all over… they treat a joke as a serious thing and a serious thing as a joke.

Sean O'Casey

To succeed in life, you need three things: a wishbone, a backbone and a funny bone.

Reba McEntire

Change your thoughts
and you change
your world.

Norman Vincent Peale

Our greatest glory is not in
never falling, but in rising
every time we fall.

Confucius

Be happy. It's one way
of being wise.

Colette

Our Irish blunders are never
blunders of the heart.

**Maria Edgeworth**

Life is 'trying things to see if they work'.

Ray Bradbury

If only we'd stop trying
to be happy we'd have a
pretty good time.

**Edith Wharton**

Birds sing after
a storm. Why
shouldn't we?

Rose Fitzgerald Kennedy

Bad times have a scientific
value. These are occasions
a good learner would
not miss.

Ralph Waldo Emerson

It is an ancient land,
honoured in the archives
of civilisation... Every great
European race has sent its
stream to the river of
the Irish mind.

**Thomas Davis,**
*Literary and Historical Essays*

When you come to
a roadblock, take
a detour.

**Mary Kay Ash**

Ah, Ireland… that
damnable, delightful
country, where everything
that is right is the opposite
of what it ought to be.

**Benjamin Disraeli**

I wouldn't mind the
rain if it wasn't
for the wet.

Jim Shanahan

The darkest hour has
only sixty minutes.

Morris Mandel

If you're already walking
on thin ice, you might
as well dance.

Proverb

The only way of preventing
what is past is to put a stop
to it before it happens.

Sir Boyle Roche

Ireland is a great country to die or be married in.

**Elizabeth Bowen**

Happiness makes
up in height what it
lacks in length.

**Robert Frost**

May you have warm words on a cold evening, a full moon on a dark night, and the road downhill all the way to your door.

**Irish blessing**

You cannot perceive
beauty but with a
serene mind.

Henry David Thoreau

If we had no winter, the
spring would not be
so pleasant; if we did
not sometimes taste of
adversity, prosperity would
not be so welcome.

Anne Bradstreet

Do not resent growing
old. Many are denied
the privilege.

**Anonymous**

He that can have
patience can have
what he will.

Benjamin Franklin

Rule number one is,
don't sweat the small
stuff. Rule number two
is, it's all small stuff.

Robert Eliot

Only Irish coffee provides
in a single glass all four
essential food groups:
alcohol, caffeine, sugar
and fat.

**Alex Levine**

An Irishman was asked if
the Irish always answered
one question with another.
'Who told you that?'
he replied.

**Niall Toibin**

# Life is simple,
# it's just not easy.

**Anonymous**

If you don't think every
day is a good day, just try
missing one.

Cavett Robert

# Melodious is the closed mouth.

**Irish proverb**

If I had my life to live over,
I would perhaps have more
actual troubles, but I'd have
fewer imaginary ones.

Don Herold

Life isn't about finding yourself. Life is about creating yourself.

George Bernard Shaw

Ever tried. Ever failed.
No matter. Try again.
Fail again. Fail better.

Samuel Beckett, *Worstwood Ho*

Obstacles are those frightful
things you see when you
take your eyes off your goal.

**Henry Ford**

Life is a shipwreck,
but we must not forget
to sing in the lifeboats.

Voltaire

Always forgive your
enemies; nothing annoys
them so much.

Oscar Wilde

The greater the
difficulty, the greater
the glory.

Marcus Tullius Cicero

Here's to eyes in your heads
and none in your spuds.

**Irish toast**

Once kick the world,
and the world and
you will live together
at a reasonably good
understanding.

Jonathan Swift

The life of man is a journey; a journey that must be travelled, however bad the roads or the accommodation.

Oliver Goldsmith

Life appears to me
too short to be spent in
nursing animosity, or
registering wrongs.

**Charlotte Brontë**, *Jane Eyre*

God is good to the
Irish, but no one else
is; not even the Irish.

**Anonymous**

Our life is what our
thoughts make it.

**Marcus Aurelius**

Life only demands from you
the strength you possess.
Only one feat is possible –
not to run away.

**Dag Hammarskjöld**

What whiskey will not cure,
there is no cure for.

**Irish proverb**

# All great achievements require time.

Maya Angelou

When I hear somebody sigh,
'Life is hard', I am always
tempted to ask, 'Compared
to what?'

Sydney J. Harris

He who knows that
enough is enough will
always have enough.

Lao Tzu

We are all in the
gutter but some of
us are looking at
the stars.

Oscar Wilde

There's a saying among prospectors: 'Go out looking for one thing and that's all you'll ever find.'

Robert J. Flaherty

It's not that the Irish are
cynical. It's rather that they
have a wonderful lack of
respect for everything
and everybody.

Brendan Behan

You never miss the
water till the well
has run dry.

**Irish proverb**

Dread of disaster makes
everybody act in the very
way that increases
the disaster.

**Bertrand Russell**

Not a shred of
evidence exists in
favour of the idea that
life is serious.

Brendan Gill

Quaintest thoughts,
queerest fancies come to
life and fade away.
What care I how time
advances? I am drinking
ale today.

Edgar Allan Poe

Today's newspaper
is tomorrow's
toilet paper.

**Barry Fitzgerald**

The question of whether
the glass is half full or half
empty depends on whether
you're drinking or pouring.

**Richard Harris**

The day after
tomorrow is the third
day of the rest of
your life.

George Carlin

My way of joking is to tell the truth. It is the funniest joke in the world.

George Bernard Shaw

I understand life isn't fair,
but why couldn't it just once
be unfair in my favour?

Christy Murphy

A dose of adversity is often as needful as a dose of medicine.

Proverb

It's not how you deal
with success that defines
you, but how you deal
with failure.

**Claire Byrne**

A good beginning is
half the work.

Irish proverb

Real difficulties can be overcome, it is only the imaginary ones that are unconquerable.

Theodore N. Vail

Become a possibilitarian.
No matter how dark things
seem or actually are, raise
your sights and see the
possibilities.

**Norman Vincent Peale**

If you can find a path
with no obstacles, it
probably doesn't lead
anywhere.

Frank A. Clark

May the roof above us
never fall in, and may we
friends gathered below
never fall out.

**Irish toast**

Blessed is he who
expects nothing, for
he shall never be
disappointed.

Jonathan Swift

The only thing experience teaches us is that experience teaches us nothing.

**André Maurois**

If one could only teach the
English how to talk, and the
Irish how to listen, society
would be quite civilised.

Oscar Wilde

Count your joys instead
of your woes; count your
friends instead of your foes.

**Irish saying**

This life is not
for complaint, but
for satisfaction.

Henry David Thoreau

I am persuaded that every time a man smiles – but much more so when he laughs – it adds something to this fragment of life.

**Laurence Sterne**

The difference
between stumbling
blocks and stepping
stones is how you
use them.

**Anonymous**

Believe not each
accusing tongue,
As most weak persons do;
But still believe that
story wrong,
Which ought not to be true!

**Richard Brinsley Sheridan**

There's naught, no
doubt, so much the
spirit calms as rum
and true religion.

Lord Byron

It's my rule never to lose
me temper till it would be
detrimental to keep it.

Sean O'Casey,
*The Plough and the Stars*

Nothing happens to
any man which he is
not formed by nature
to bear.

**Marcus Aurelius**

Never be afraid to try.
Remember: amateurs built
the ark, professionals built
the *Titanic*.

**Anonymous**

A peaceful man does
more good than a
learned one.

**Pope John XXIII**

I am not afraid of tomorrow,
for I have seen yesterday
and I love today.

William Allen White

All the world's a
stage and most of
us are desperately
unrehearsed.

Sean O'Casey

Nobody made a greater
mistake than he who did
nothing because he could
only do a little.

Edmund Burke

# Happiness is not a goal, it's a by-product.

**Eleanor Roosevelt**

We act as though comfort
and luxury were the chief
requirements of life, when
all we need to make us
really happy is something to
be enthusiastic about.

**Charles Kingsley**

Be nice to people on
your way up because
you'll meet 'em on
your way down.

**Wilson Mizner**

Firelight will not let
you read fine stories,
but it's warm, and you
won't see the dust on
the floor.

**Irish saying**

Let us have wine and
women, mirth and laughter,
Sermons and soda-water
the day after.

**Lord Byron**

I woke up this morning
and I'm still alive, so
I'm pretty cheerful.

**Spike Milligan**

Wherever you go and
whatever you do,
May the luck of the Irish be
there with you.

**Irish blessing**

# KEEP CALM
# AND
# DRINK UP

£4.99

ISBN: 978-1-84953-102-3

*'In victory, you deserve champagne;
in defeat, you need it.'*

Napoleon Bonaparte

## BAD ADVICE FOR GOOD PEOPLE

Keep Calm and Carry On, a World War Two government poster, struck a chord in recent difficult times when a stiff upper lip and optimistic energy were needed again. But in the long run it's a stiff drink and flowing spirits that keep us all going.

Here's a book packed with proverbs and quotations showing the wisdom to be found at the bottom of the glass.

# NOW PANIC
# AND
# FREAK OUT

£4.99

ISBN: 978-1-84953-103-0

*'We experience moments absolutely free from worry. These brief respites are called panic.'*

Cullen Hightower

## BAD ADVICE FOR GOOD PEOPLE

Keep Calm and Carry On is all very well, but life just isn't that simple. Let's own up and face facts: we're getting older, the politicians are not getting any wiser, and the world's going to hell in a handbasket.

It's time to panic.

Here's a book packed with quotations proving that keeping calm is simply not an option.

If you're interested in finding out
more about our humour books, follow us
on Twitter: @SummersdaleLOL


**www.summersdale.com**